CHEAP SHOTS

AN INCREDIBLY INEXPENSIVE COLLECTION OF POLITICAL CARTOONS BY MIKE THOMPSON

The State Journal-Register

Library of Congress Catalog Card Number:
96-96959

ISBN:
0-9653765-0-8

Printed by Phillips Brothers Printers
Springfield, Illinois

INTRODUCTION

Well, let's get right to the bottom line. Mike Thompson, the incredibly gifted editorial cartoonist for The State Journal-Register, has gathered together a great collection of his cartoons for publication to a wider audience. The cartoons are funny, insightful and often wickedly on target. Most importantly, he never drew a bad picture of me. A little more hair and a little less chin would have been nice, but maybe he's a Democrat.

The cartoons range from the not-so-gentle skewering of Jesse Jackson's rhyming rhetoric to a reminder that those who don't like Bob Dole or his campaign would have trashed Abe Lincoln, too. In this delightful compilation, Bill Clinton is transformed rhetorically into Ronald Reagan (except, of course, Reagan believed it!).

Satirical and political cartooning have an ancient and honorable pedigree. Lawyers decorate their offices with Daumier engravings while their younger associates (a decade and a lifestyle away) discreetly personalize "Dilbert" for the men's room. And every politician who has felt the sting of Thompson and his cohorts can also feel a comparative sense of relief that they were not the targets of the predators that circled the campaigns of 19th-century politicians like Old Abe and the Tammany gang.

Why are political cartoons important in 20th-century politics? Because they can convey a single idea in a split-second glance. Appraisal, recognition, reaction and impression all come in an instant, in the same way that a defining television moment does. For a public that is increasingly skeptical -- and weary -- of politicians, for those who refuse to wade though lengthy news analyses or sit through windy political addresses, the Mike Thompsons of the world can deliver it all, painlessly and humorously (for the reader).

What a deal!

James R. Thompson
Governor of Illinois
1977-1991

I'd like to thank all the people who helped me put out this book. Special thanks to Connie, Pat Coburn, David Ahntholz, Steve Fagan, Jack Clarke, Barry Locher, Chris Young, Colleen Roate, and The State Journal-Register camera-plate department.

-Mike Thompson, Oct. 1, 1996

CONTENTS:

CAMPAIN '96

STOP KIDS' SMOKING...

..END TEEN PREGNANCIES...

..TAX CREDITS FOR ADOPTIONS

..CUT WELFARE...

..SAY NO TO DRUGS...

...JELLYBEAN, ANYONE?

13

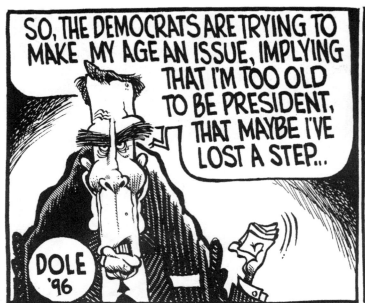

"COLIN POWELL SHOWERED THIS MORNING—FOR AN IN-DEPTH ANALYSIS OF HOW THIS LATEST DEVELOPMENT WILL IMPACT THE DOLE CANDIDACY, WE GO TO WOLF BLITZER!..."

17

THE ONLY FORBES THAT WILL EVER GET INTO THE WHITE HOUSE

"BOY, CLINTON'S HAVING AN UNUSUALLY SLOW DAY... IT'S TWO HOURS 'TIL NOON AND HE'S **YET** TO BECOME EMBROILED IN A MAJOR SCANDAL ..."

24

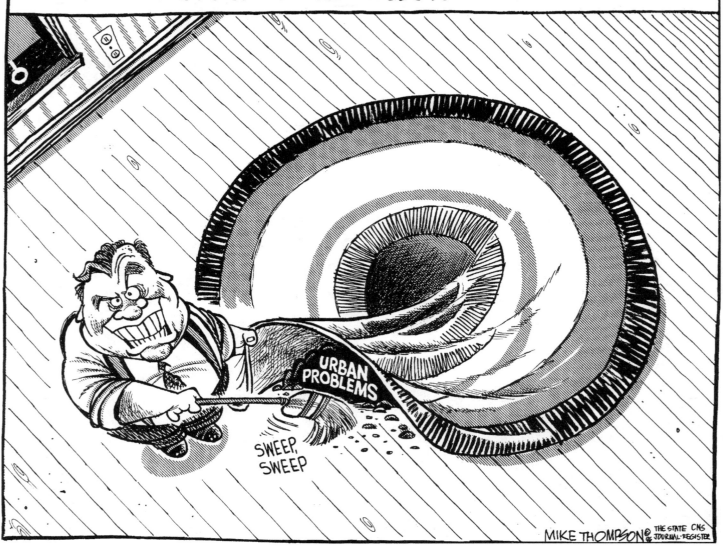

26

Symbols of Illinois:

STATE MOTTO:

STATE ROCK:

STATE TREE:

STATE "BIRD":

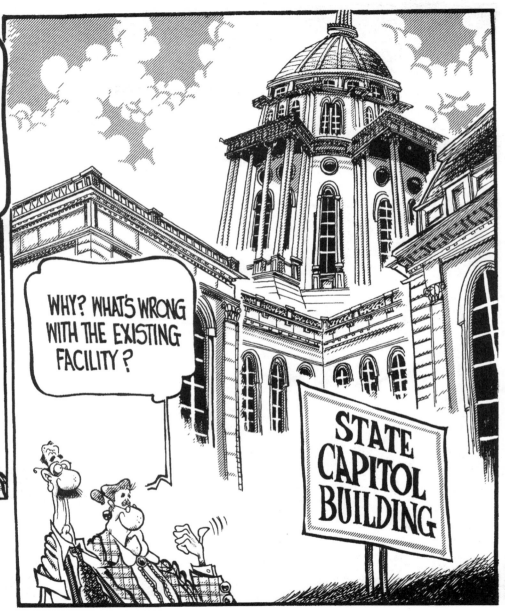

The Hanging Judge

41

43

The Speech Process of Pate Philip:

THE BRAIN

THE GUT

MIKE THOMPSON © THE STATE JOURNAL - REGISTER
'93 COPLEY NEWS SERVICE

44

45

I'VE TRAVELED ILLINOIS TO MAKE **NOISE** ABOUT EDGAR AN' HIS **BOYS**!...

JESSE'S FREEDOM TOUR

AND THE REPUBLICAN **PLAN** TO HURT THE WORKING **MAN** LIKE AN **AFGHAN** ON AN **OTTOMAN**!!

THEY'LL BRING YA TO YOUR **KNEES**, BEGGIN' **PLEASE** LIKE THE **PORTUGUESE** IN A **SQUEEZE**!!

THEY'LL PUT YOU **DOWN** LIKE A **CLOWN** IN A **SHOWDOWN** IN **CHINATOWN**!!

LIKE A **SCRUNGE** OF A **SPONGE** DRESSED IN **GRUNGE** EATING **MUSKELLUNGE**!!

IF YOU GET MY POINT.

Mike Thompson © THE STATE JOURNAL-REGISTER/CNS

47

48

Dan Rostenkowski's Punishment:

DETAILED EXPLANATION:

CORRUPTION CHARGES → 13 COUNTS!

↓

PLEA BARGAIN

↓

$100,000 FINE
+
17-MONTH PRISON SENTENCE
(How much will actually be served?)

(TAXPAYERS OUT $700,000.00)

SIMPLIFIED EXPLANATION:

SLAP HERE

49

50

Chicago Politics

THEN:
DEAD MEN ARE
IMPORTANT POLITICAL PLAYERS

I VOTED

I VOTED

I VOTED

I VOTED

NOW:
IMPORTANT POLITICAL PLAYERS ARE
DEAD MEN

MEL
REYNOLDS

ROSTENKOWSKI

INDICTMENTS

MIKE THOMPSON © '94 THE STATE-JOURNAL-REGISTER / CNS

The Running of the Bulls

ED the Daredevil!

THRILL-SEEKER WHO CRAVES DANGER!!

SCALES PERILOUS MOUNTAINS!..

...SWIMS PIRANHA-INFESTED RIVERS!..

...LEAPS GIANT POOLS OF MOLTEN LAVA!..

...FLIES INTO CHICAGO O'HARE AIRPORT!

RADAR? **WHAT** RADAR?!

MIKE THOMPSON ©95
THE STATE JOURNAL-REGISTER
COPLEY NEWS SERVICE

the
TEFLON GOVERNOR

the
VELCRO CHALLENGER

58

60

"BEFORE I BEGIN, I'D LIKE TO REQUEST THAT DAWN CLARK NETSCH, WHEREVER SHE IS, WIPE THAT BIG OL' SMUG SMIRK OFF HER FACE!.."

69

Q: WHAT'S THE ONLY THING MORE COSTLY THAN THE HIGH PRICE OF REFORMING DCFS?

A: THE HIGH PRICE OF NOT REFORMING DCFS

news

MILLIONS NEEDED FOR DCFS REFORMS

JOSEPH WALLACE

AGE 3

MIKE THOMPSON © THE STATE JOURNAL-REGISTER
93 COPLEY NEWS SERVICE

73

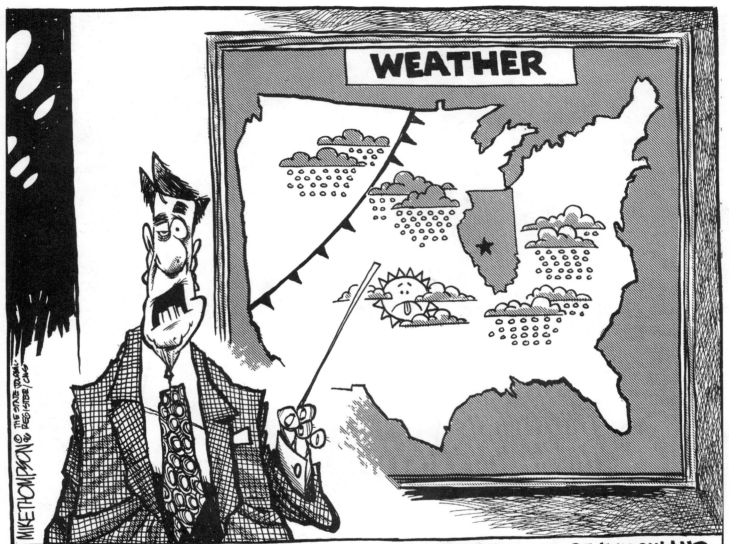

"EXPECT CONTINUED 'BLEEEECH!' FOLLOWED BY PATCHES OF 'YUCK' AND 'YEEESH' WITH 'UUUUGH!' AND 'YEEEW!' CONTINUING THROUGH TOMORROW..."

LIFE IN AMERICA

FIRST THERE WERE TELEPHONES.

THEN THERE WAS CALL WAITING AND ANSWERING MACHINES.

THEN CAME CALL FORWARDING, FAX MACHINES, VOICE MAIL, MODEMS, CAR PHONES, CAR FAXES, BEEPERS AND FINALLY PERSONALIZED "1-700" NUMBERS.

THOMPSON © '92
THE STATE JOURNAL-REGISTER
COPLEY NEWS SERVICE

NOW, **ANYONE** CAN BE REACHED BY **ANYONE** ELSE, **ANYHOW**, **ANYWHERE**, **ANY TIME** OF DAY OR NIGHT FOR **ANY** REASON,

GOOD GOD! **WHAT** HAVE WE DONE?!!

The Inaccurate Conception

80

84

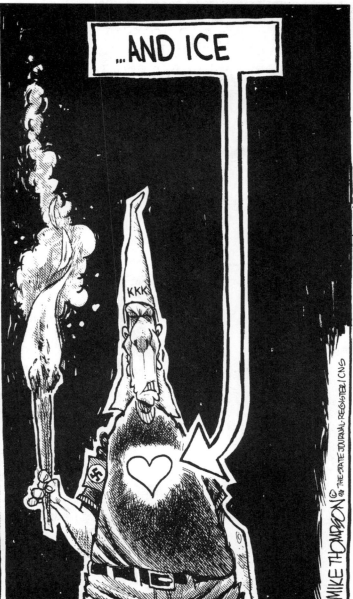

90

The most pathetic sight in all of Washington...

...An electioneering Congressman Kissing 'butt'...

95

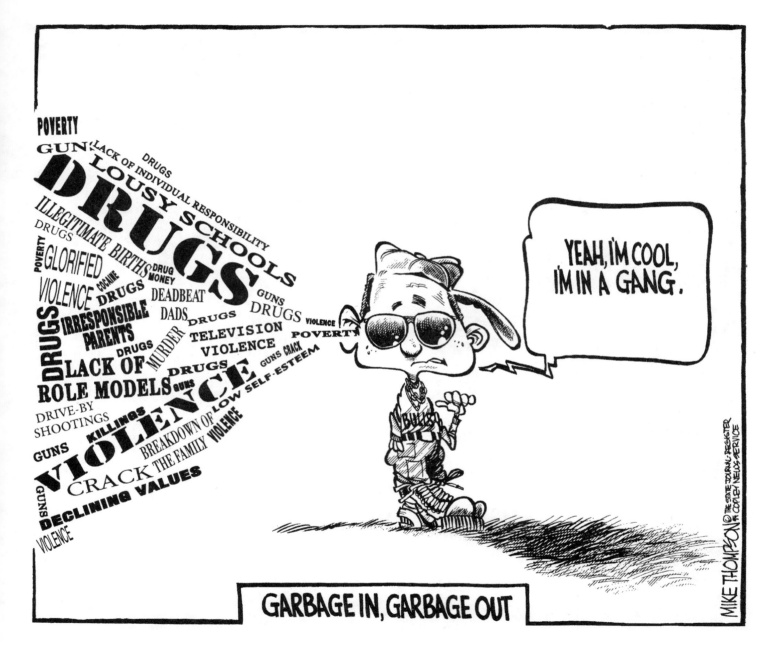

Reasons to Join a Gang:

① THE NEW FASHIONS YOU'LL BE SPORTING!:

PROPERTY OF COUNTY JAIL

② YOUR DOINGS WILL BE FRONT PAGE NEWS!:

THE NEWS
GANG MEMBER ARRESTED

News
GANG MEMBER SHOT, KILLED

③ THE COOL JEWELRY YOU'LL BE WEARING!:

④ INCREASE YOUR PROFILE!:

⑤ BE SEEN RIDING AROUND IN REALLY BIG, SHINY CARS!:

HEARSE

⑥ EARN A PERMANENT SPOT AMONG A NEW PEER GROUP!:

RIP RIP RIP

MIKE THOMPSON© '94 THE STATE JOURNAL-REGISTER / CNS

THE SECRETARY OF STATE OF CONFUSION

100

103

MTV
PRESENTS
WHEN I ASKED MTV FOR A SHOW AND A ROLE THAT WOULD MATCH MY PERSONALITY, THIS AIN'T WHAT I HAD IN MIND...
RODMAN
BEAVIS
AND
BUTT-HEAD
MIKE THOMPSON © '96 (APOLOGIES TO MTV)
THE STATE JOURNAL-REGISTER
COPLEY NEWS SERVICE

107

109

MAINSTREAM VALUES

MOVIE INDUSTRY

PLANET HOLLYWOOD

113

An 'Abbreviated' History of Social Programs:

THE MICHIGAN MILITIA DOES LAUNDRY

116

125

If Professionals Were Paid What They Were Truly Worth:

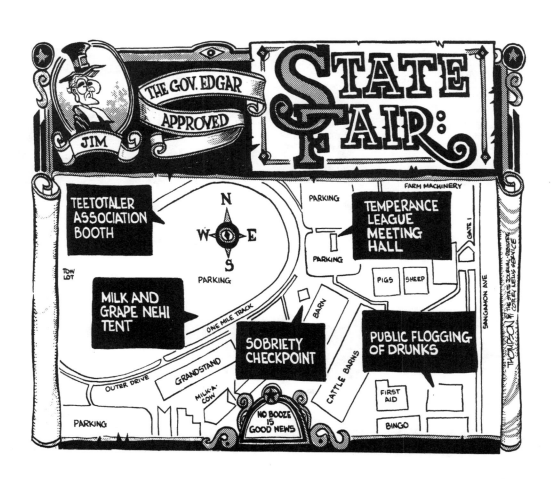

DEFINITIVE PROOF THAT MANAGEMENT OF THE SHA HAS BEEN REALLY, **REALLY** BAD :
IT AIN'T EVEN UP TO **MY** STANDARDS...
THE FEDERAL GOVERNMENT
SHA TAKEOVER
MIKE THOMPSON © 96
THE STATE JOURNAL-REGISTER

139

GIVE SOMEONE A CHEAP SHOT!

Order someone a copy of "CHEAP SHOTS, an incredibly inexpensive collection of political cartoons by Mike Thompson." Or, order another copy for yourself! Just clip, fill out and mail the form below:

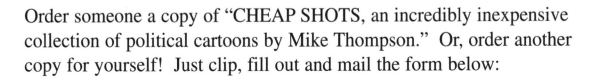

Please send me _____ copies of **CHEAP SHOTS** by Mike Thompson

$6.95 each book = _____

$3.00 shipping & handling per book=_____

$_____= Total

Make check payable and mail to:

The State Journal-Register
Promotion Department / book order
1 Copley Plaza, Springfield, IL 62705-0219

Mail book(s) to:

Name_____Telephone_____

Address_____

City_____State_____Zip_____